GREAT INVENTIONS

THE STEAM ENGINE

By Deborah DeFord

WORLD ALMANAC® LIBRARY

Please visit our web site at: www.worldalmanaclibrary.com
For a free color catalog describing World Almanac® Library's list of high-quality books
and multimedia programs, call 1-800-848-2928 (USA) or 1-800-387-3178 (Canada).
World Almanac® Library's fax: (414) 332-3567.

Library of Congress Cataloging-in-Publication Data

DeFord, Deborah H.
    The steam engine / by Deborah DeFord.
      p. cm. — (Great inventions)
    Includes bibliographical references and index.
    ISBN 0-8368-5803-4 (lib. bdg.)
    ISBN 0-8368-6590-1 (softcover)
      1. Steam engines—Juvenile literature. I. Title.
  TJ467.D44   2005
  621.1—dc22   2004061599

First published in 2005 by
World Almanac® Library
330 West Olive Street, Suite 100
Milwaukee, WI 53132 USA

A Creative Media Applications, Inc. Production
Design and Production: Alan Barnett, Inc.
Editors: Matt Levine, Susan Madoff
Copy Editor: Laurie Lieb
Proofreader: Laurie Lieb
Indexer: Nara Wood
World Almanac® Library editorial direction: Mark J. Sachner
World Almanac® Library editor: Gini Holland
World Almanac® Library art direction: Tammy West
World Almanac® Library production: Jessica Morris

Photo credits: © AP/Wide World Photos: pages 29, 41, 42; © Bettmann/CORBIS: pages 10,
13, 14, 20, 30, 34; ClipArt.com: pages 9, 11, 12, 17, 18, 23, 24, 27, 32, 33, 38; © Getty
Images/Hulton Archive: pages 6, 37; The Granger Collection, New York: page 26
© Hulton-Deutsch Collection/CORBIS: page 22; © Jim Zuckerman/CORBIS: page 8;
© North Wind Picture Archives: page 4; Photos.com: page 38; diagram by Rolin Graphics:
page 18

Printed in the United States of America

1 2 3 4 5 6 7 8 9 09 08 07 06 05

TABLE OF CONTENTS

Words that appear in the glossary are printed in
boldface type the first time they appear in the text.

1

TURNING STEAM INTO POWER

▼ Hero's aeolipile, the earliest recorded steam device, designed to spin a toy ball, was built in the first century.

Imagine a world with no engines. Land travel would slow down to the speed traveled by a person on foot or on horseback. Ships would sail only when the wind blew. If there were no engines, factories would stop running if the wind failed to blow or water ran dry. Electric generation plants would not be able to produce a constant flow of electricity. Millions of homes and businesses would have to do without lights, appliances, televisions, computers, and central heating and cooling systems. When the first steam engines were invented, inventors did not realize their great potential for solving practical problems of everyday life. They couldn't even fathom that the day would come when people would depend on engines for nearly all the work, play, travel, and communicating they do. The inventors only wanted to create a device that could convert fuel **energy** into **mechanical work.**

The potential for steam power has always been available, wherever water and heat could be found. It took people tens of thousands of years, though, to discover how to harness that power and use steam to change their world. When someone imagined using steam to power an **engine**, a mighty and constant source of energy was revealed. This was power human beings could control, unlike water or wind that came and went at the whim of nature. Also, steam was a potential force that would not grow tired, the way people and animals do. Recognizing the power of steam was the first step toward modernizing our way of life.

Early Experiments

The first people to understand the power of steam were not trying to build engines. Hero of Alexandria, a Greek mathematician and scientist in the first century A.D., created the earliest steam devices recorded

The Secret of the Temple Doors

The ancient Greeks apparently used steam power to work some impressive special effects. The Greeks believed in many gods, and the Greek practice of religion was often mixed up with a fair amount of magic and superstition. In his writings, Hero of Alexandria revealed how the priests created one illusion that kept their temples full of worshippers. The priests would light a fire outside the temple doors as a ritual offering to please the gods. Unbeknown to the people who watched, the fire was actually heating a closed container of moist air. The heat produced steam, which expanded beyond its container through a tube to another container full of water. The expanding steam pushed some of the water out through another tube that emptied into a bucket. The bucket, hidden from the worshippers' view, was attached to a rope that ran over a pulley and attached at the other end to the temple doors. As the bucket filled with water, it grew heavier and pulled the rope, which in turned opened the temple doors. To the watching crowd, it seemed as if the doors opened by themselves. The priests interpreted this as the gods' way of accepting the people's fire offering.

in history. His most famous invention, called an *aeolipile*, was actually a globe-shaped toy that would spin rapidly under steam power.

Over hundreds of years, people experimented with steam, observing the way it expanded and built up **pressure** in a closed container until the steam whistled out of openings and made pot lids rattle. They saw that as steam cooled in a tightly covered container, the cover became harder to remove. Each new experiment gave inventors new ideas about how steam could be converted into mechanical force.

In 1602, an Italian mathematician named Giovanni Bettista della Porta (1538–1615) developed an idea to use the expansion property of steam to create a water fountain. While he was working on this theory, he recognized that cooling steam actually created a vacuum that might be used to raise liquid in the same way a person sucks up water through a straw. This observation would later be important information in developing a modern steam engine.

Another inventor, Edward Somerset (1601–1675) of England obtained a ninety-nine-year **patent** from the British government for a steam engine that could raise water from a castle moat to its towers. Somerset, who lived in a castle himself, called his invention a "Watercommanding Engine" and claimed that the device might also work to drain the water that flooded a marshland or the depths of a coal mine.

None of these inventors invented the steam engine that would later revolutionize

▼ Edward Somerset's "Watercommanding Engine" raised water from a moat surrounding his castle. Somerset's interest in the invention of garden fountains spurred his curiosity about using steam as a way to power a water pump.

The Steam Engine

people's lives. Yet each of their experiments and successes was an important step leading to the great accomplishment of later inventors—capturing the vast potential of steam power.

The Power of Steam

Steam is a pure, invisible gas that is created when water is heated above the boiling point. Steam takes up about 1,600 times as much space as the water that produced it. This means that if water is heated to form steam in a closed container, the steam will eventually take up more space than the container can provide.

The more steam there is, the greater the force it exerts on the walls of a container. This force is called pressure, and when the pressure reaches a high enough level, the steam will jet-propel out of any and all openings in the container. Think of what happens, for example, when water boils in a whistling teakettle. That whistle is produced by steam venting out of the whistle hole.

Inventors experimented with steam because they needed a reliable source of energy to accomplish

Blowing Its Top Off

In the spring of 1980, in the Cascade Mountains of Washington, a sleeping volcano called Mount St. Helens came to life. People living in the region felt the first signs of what was to come when a series of small earthquakes rattled dishes and made floors vibrate. Meanwhile, under the earth's surface, water was being shaken into contact with the hot molten rock at Mount St. Helens's core. The extreme heat turned the water to steam, which expanded to the point that the steam pressure could no longer be contained. The steam power was so monumental that it blasted the top off the mountain, spewing rock, ash, and glacial ice, leaving a gigantic crater in its place.

work. People once relied on the energy available in their own muscles or the muscles of animals such as horses and oxen to do their work. At some point, during the Stone Age, they learned to make and use tools. Over time, their tools became more elaborate and were turned into **machines** with moving parts. These machines made it possible to do more and harder work with less effort. The machines, however, still needed some kind of energy, or engine, to run them. Inventors realized that wind or water could drive a mill wheel that would in turn operate a machine, but wind and water depended on forces of nature that people could not control.

Steam, as people discovered, provided a predictable, reliable source of energy. Once steam's properties of expansion and condensation were understood, it was only a matter of time before scientists with plenty of curiosity and imagination figured out how to put it to good use.

The Steam Engine

STEAM-DRIVEN MACHINES

By the late 1600s, people were working hard to invent processes to do old jobs in newer, faster, and more economical ways. In England especially, where prosperity had created new demands for fuel and goods, more and more mines were being dug for needed minerals and coal. At the same time, mills for sawing wood, grinding grain, spinning thread, and weaving fabric were popping up wherever rivers provided power for waterwheels.

One of the country's biggest challenges at the time was removing water from England's many mines. As miners dug deep holes in the ground to remove coal, copper, and tin for various uses, groundwater would seep into the mine shafts, making it impossible to continue mining the depths. Without engines, draining the mines was a slow, hand- or horse-driven business. Several inventors and engineers put their minds to solving this water-removal problem. Before long, they decided that steam power was the answer.

In the 1690s, a scientist named Denis Papin decided to try using the vacuum produced by cooling steam to develop a steam engine. He began with a small brass **cylinder** about 2.5 inches (6.4 centimeters) in diameter. In the bottom of the cylinder, Papin poured a small amount of water. He then inserted a **piston**, or rod, that fit snugly into the cylinder. At the top of the piston he

▼ *This photograph shows Denis Papin's experiment, which used a cylinder and piston to illustrate the power of steam.*

Denis Papin (1647–1712)

Denis Papin was born in 1647 in France, where he received medical training that he would soon put to use in scientific experiments. In London, Papin became a Fellow of the Royal Society. Papin worked for a British scientist named Robert Boyle. In Boyle's laboratory, Papin developed an air pump that depended on steam and the vacuum produced by condensing steam. He also invented "a new Digester and Engine for softening Bones," which people today consider to be the first steam pressure cooker. His "digester" employed the first steam safety valve. At the same time, he created the first model of a steam engine that used a piston in a cylinder. Papin died a poor man in 1712 at the age of sixty-seven.

attached a cord that ran over a pulley and was attached to a weight at the other end.

Finally, Papin put the cylinder over a fire and brought the water in the cylinder to a boil. As steam formed, it expanded, forcing the piston to rise to the top of the cylinder, where it was caught and held by a catch. When Papin removed the fire, the steam cooled and condensed, forming a partial vacuum. He then removed the catch. The piston was sucked back down with such force that it lifted 60 pounds (27 kilograms) of weight attached to the other end of the cord.

Papin's experiment showed that steam could be used to run an engine that was more powerful than any animal power source could provide. He lacked the technical know-how, however, to turn his experiment into a functioning engine. When he later tried to build a full-size piston engine, his project failed. Papin lost interest and moved on to other kinds of experiments.

The Miner's Friend

Other inventors and engineers did not give up on steam. Papin's idea was made more practical by an Englishman named Thomas Savery. Savery obtained a patent from the English government in 1698 for "a new Invention for Raising of Water and occasioning Motion to all sorts of Mill Work by the Impellent Force of Fire." As Savery explained, this invention would "be of great Use and Advantage for Draining Mines, serving Towns with Water, and for the Working of all Sort of Mills where they have not the Benefit of Water nor Constant Winds." To prove his point, Savery built a 58-foot (17.6-meter) water lift that ran on steam, working on principles earlier described by della Porta. His lift could pump 3,000 gallons (11,355 liters) of water in an hour.

In Savery's pump, steam from a boiler passed into a closed container filled with water. The steam pressure forced the water up through an ascending pipe fitted with a nonreturn valve that kept the water from flowing back through the pipe. When all the water was forced out of the container, the steam was shut off by hand and cold water was run over the container to cool the steam that now filled it. As the steam condensed, it formed a vacuum in the container, which pulled water up through a suction pipe. Once the container had filled, the flow of cold water on the outside of the container was turned off, the steam turned back on, and the cycle repeated.

In 1702, Savery set up the world's first steam pump manufacturing shop in London, preparing to sell his pumps to mines throughout Britain. Like Papin, however, he ran into technical difficulties he did not know how to solve. The mine shafts could be 200 or 300 feet (61 or 92 m) deep, and Savery's engine could not raise water more than 25 feet (7.6 m) before the air pressure, or atmospheric pressure, stopped it. His engines created so much heat and steam pressure that they sometimes melted or split the pumps' seams and joints. In addition, his engines had to burn a huge, costly amount of coal in order to continuously reheat the water and create the steam.

Although Savery's pump did not work particularly well, he still owned a patent that applied to almost any device using steam to pump water. When another inventor named Thomas Newcomen figured out a better way to build and sell a steam engine, he was in danger of violating Savery's exclusive right to create steam engines for sale. Newcomen decided to make Savery a partner in the business.

Thomas Savery (1650–1715)

Thomas Savery was born in the tin- and copper-mining region of England in 1650 and died in 1715. He under-stood the need for powerful pumps that could drain water from mines. He obtained numerous patents for experiments with steam-powered pumps, including one for "an engine to raise water by fire" in 1698. By 1699, he had made the first successful demonstra-tion of a steam engine pump to the Royal Society. Savery's pumps for mine drainage ran into technical troubles, however, and one of his boilers (used to convert water to steam) pro-duced the first recorded boiler explosion.

Early patents were exclusive rights given by a government to an inventor for a technological advance. Today, patents protect ownership rights to a product. The earliest patent on record was granted by Henry VI in 1449 for a process to create stained glass. In America, Thomas Jefferson was influential in developing an official patent system in 1790. Modern patent law is largely the same system, although it was restructured in 1836. Nowadays, however, new technology develops before a patent is even granted. Our rapidly changing world calls for an update to the patent system to promote scientific advancement.

▶ *Thomas Newcomen's atmospheric engine improved upon Thomas Savery's steam pump by using the vacuum created by the steam cycle.*

The Atmospheric Engine

It took Thomas Newcomen ten years of trial and error to develop a steam engine that would actually work to remove water from deep within the mines. Throughout that time, he built all his experimental steam engines as models on a small scale. When problems occurred, he kept trying solutions until he found one that worked.

Newcomen's engine used a boiler, a piston in a cylinder like Papin's, and a beam that rocked on a pivot point like a seesaw to create mechanical force. Unlike Savery's device, Newcomen's engine did not serve as the pump. Instead, it was used to drive a

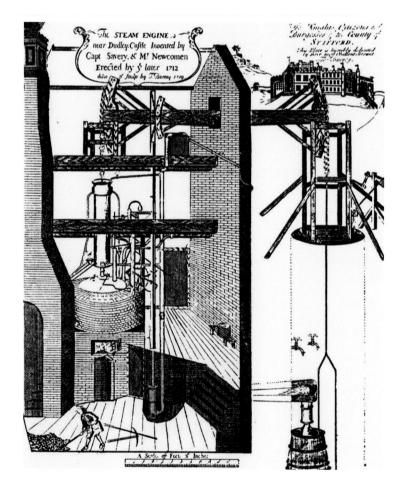

The STEAM ENGINE near Dudley Castle Invented by Capt Savery, & Mr Newcomen Erected by ye later 1712

separate pump that would have otherwise been driven by horse or wind power. Newcomen's invention became the first true engine run on steam.

Newcomen solved Savery's problems with boiler explosions and meltdowns by using only the condensation, or vacuum, part of the steam cycle to power his engine. This eliminated the need for the high steam pressure that could push the piston upward. The piston was raised by the weight of the beam and allowed steam to fill the cylinder beneath it. When the steam pressure equaled the atmospheric pressure outside the engine, the steam valve was closed. When the steam condensed and created the vacuum, the atmospheric pressure would push the piston down with force. (For this reason, the engine is often called an atmospheric engine.)

Newcomen improved the vacuum efficiency of the piston and cylinder by creating a seal of leather and water at the top of the piston that kept air from entering around its edges. It was an accident, however, that led to Newcomen's greatest improvement. When the engine's cylinder developed a hole that let cold water leak in, the steam condensed much more quickly, greatly increasing the force of the piston. Newcomen then modified the engine so that cool water could be injected directly into the steam chamber instead of being poured over the outside of the chamber. That change made his steam engine much more powerful.

With Newcomen's improvements, the age of the steam engine was launched. Newcomen had found answers to problems that had plagued inventors for many years before him. He set the stage for other inventors whose improvements to the steam engine would thrust the world toward what would eventually be called the Industrial Revolution.

Thomas Newcomen (1663–1729)

Thomas Newcomen was born in 1663 in England. His experience as an ironmaster (a manufacturer of iron) gave him an insider's knowledge of the problem of groundwater filling the tin mines of his region. He developed a steam-powered pump that could drain the water from the mines more quickly than the horse-driven pumps of the time. In 1698, he joined forces with Thomas Savery. Under Savery's steam engine patent, Newcomen was able to manufacture his first full-scale engine in 1712. Eventually, he invented the first steam engine that could be commercially operated for a reasonable cost. By 1755, Newcomen's engines were in wide use in Europe and even North Africa.

3 MAJOR IMPROVEMENTS

▼ *James Watt's childhood interest in steam power was inspired by his fascination with a tea kettle and the way it produced pressure and steam. This undated engraving is titled* James Watt's First Experiment.

The British Isles were bustling with commerce by the mid-1700s. Great Britain had acquired colonies and connections around the world, which meant that the country's mills and manufacturers had a good supply of raw materials. Those same connections created plentiful markets for British goods manufactured from the raw materials. British businesses could not produce goods fast enough to meet the demands of the expanding population.

At the same time, many of the British had developed a lively interest in science, philosophy, and invention. They believed that progress depended on learning more about how things work. They were convinced, as well, that new ideas and inventions would lead to successful ventures and greater wealth for both Great Britain and its citizens.

The steam engine, as Newcomen had developed it, made a great impact during this optimistic time. The engine could pump water out of mines far more consistently and quickly than any method run on animal or natural power. It had its problems, however, including

The Industrial Revolution

The Industrial Revolution became a force that changed our world when power-driven machinery was adapted to manufacturing. Dramatic social and economic changes began taking place in England around 1733, as more and more factories, relying on the availability of steam-generated power, sprang up around the country. The increase in manufactured goods, such as textiles and household products, brought wealth to factory owners and increased the standard of living of those who left their farms and small craft shops and went to work for a steady wage in the factory. As machinery improved, workers became more productive. Prices dropped, making items once available only to the rich accessible to the lower classes. By the end of the eighteenth century, western Europe and the United States had become industrialized. Steam-powered locomotives and ships transported goods to all areas of the world, spreading the new technology of the machine age.

the fact that it took an enormous amount of coal to operate. Coal cost the mine owners a lot of money, especially if they had to transport it from a distance, and it ate up more of their profits than they liked.

Steam Power's Most Famous Inventor

By the time a young Scottish engineer named James Watt (1736-1819) came along, people were ready to replace the Newcomen steam engine with a better one. When a professor at the University of Glasgow asked Watt to repair a model of a Newcomen engine, he immediately saw what needed improvement and went to work on fixing the problems.

Legend has it that Watt had been keeping an eye on steam and its properties for some time. Even as a little boy, he had spent a lot of time watching what happened when water boiled and steamed in a teakettle over a fire. Both his grandfather and his uncle were mathematicians, and they provided him with plenty of reading on the subject.

Fast Fact

The Royal Society, founded in 1660, was an academy dedicated to excellence in science. Still in existence today, the Royal Society supported the work of many inventors. It had great influence on who received patents from the British government and even today lends its voice to debate on key scientific issues that affect the public.

Other people, too, were interested in the untapped potential of steam. Once the Savery-Newcomen patent ran out in 1733, many people legally built and sold steam engines that were economical and powerful. By the time Watt had a Newcomen model steam engine in his hands, as many as 350 different kinds of steam pumps had been built and 250 remained in operation. They did not operate better than the Newcomen engine, however. Most of the engine producers at the time simply made the old design larger, hoping to improve the engine's performance.

Problems and Solutions

In order to pursue his ideas, Watt needed financial help. So he teamed up with John Roebuck, the English director of an ironworks in Scotland. Roebuck liked the idea of an engine that would increase production in his industry. He could also see the business advantages in being the first to market an improved engine. With Roebuck's money in hand, Watt got busy figuring out how to make the Newcomen engine perform better.

Watt's initial discovery was that Newcomen's engine used up too much steam. It could not run for more than a few strokes at a time because it required that the metal cylinder be continually heated up, cooled, and reheated. This process wasted a lot of heat and steam that could have been used to keep the engine running.

Watt realized that if he could move the steam into a separate container for the steam's condensation, he could keep the cylinder constantly as hot as the steam itself. Steam would actually be produced more quickly, and the separate condenser would keep the engine running without pause.

The Steam Engine

To make the engine even more efficient, Watt next covered both ends of the cylinder and encased it in a "steam jacket" to conserve the heat. He added valves that connected the cylinder to the boiler at both ends, creating a double-acting engine. Steam was added alternately to both ends of the cylinder.

As steam in the bottom expanded, it pushed the piston up. Then steam in the top of the cylinder (instead of atmospheric pressure) pushed the piston back down as condensing steam formed the vacuum below.

By 1769, Watt had secured a patent for his improved engine. He could not stop tinkering long enough, however, to put the engine into production. Ideas for improvements kept coming to him, and he insisted on experimenting with them. Before he could finish, Roebuck had run out of money. In 1775, Watt started a new partnership, this time with a British manufacturer named Matthew Boulton. With Boulton, Watt at last allowed his new, improved steam engine design to be put into production.

▲ *James Watt secured a patent for his steam engine in 1769. He and his partner, Matthew Boulton, were the sole manufacturers of the device for the next twenty-five years.*

The Rights to Progress

Boulton decided that "if most profit" were to be made, he and Watt must secure exclusive rights to Watt's inventions. He personally went to Parliament, Great Britain's lawmaking body, and secured a twenty-five-year patent that granted Watt "the sole Use and Property of certain Steam Engines." Under

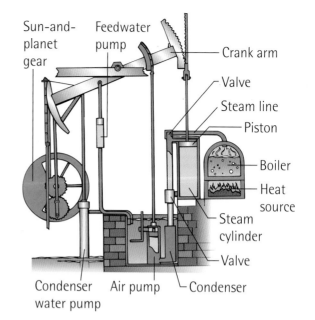

Sun-and-planet gear — Feedwater pump — Crank arm — Valve — Steam line — Piston — Boiler — Heat source — Steam cylinder — Valve — Condenser — Air pump — Condenser water pump

► *James Watt's improvement to Thomas Newcomen's steam engine rested on the use of a separate condenser that allowed the steam cylinder to remain hot at all times and increase the steam's efficiency. The condenser was connected to the cylinder through a valve. When the piston reached the top of the cylinder, the valve was closed and another opened. The steam then poured from the cylinder into the condenser, which was kept cool, and then pumped along using the air pump. This illustration of Watt's atmospheric engine shows how water was fed into the engine through a pump, heated in the boiler, and sent through the cylinder and condenser by a valve system and air pump. The sun-and-planet gear converted the motion of the piston into a circular movement that could operate machine gears.*

the patent, Boulton & Watt became the only company entitled to build steam engines. The two men further increased their earnings by charging an extra royalty, or fee, on every engine they installed. Businesses were expected to pay the fee based on how much money they saved in fuel costs by using the Watt engine instead of a Newcomen engine.

Watt's invention reflected the changes that were occurring in manufacturing, especially in Great Britain's textile mills. Unlike mines that needed engines for the up-and-down (or reciprocal) motion of a water pump, the mills required a circular action to turn the belts and gears connected to various textile machines. These machines spun cotton and wool into thread, wove thread and yarn into fabric, and washed and scoured finished cloth.

Watt's solution to the problem was a "sun-and-planet" gear that converted the reciprocal action of the piston and beam into a rotary, or circular, action that could turn a belt or set of machine gears. Once Watt had changed the motion of the engine, the ways it could be used were almost endless. Any manufacturing that was run by a waterwheel could now be freed of the rivers and seasons that dictated water flow. One of Watt's earliest installations of the rotative, or turning, steam engine ran a flour mill. With two engines in place, steam could keep twenty sets of millstones turning at once, grinding flour.

Watt, meanwhile, paid steady attention to measuring and regulating the performance of his engines. In order to provide a measurement, he compared the engine's workload to that of a strong horse. By 1782, he was describing his engines in terms of their horsepower, a term that is still used today. He sold fourteen-horse engines, twenty-horse engines, and so forth. He defined one unit of horsepower as 33,000 pounds (15,000 kg) moved 1 foot (0.3 m) in one minute.

Watt also developed a steam engine indicator that would track the movement of the engine's piston. This device actually created a pencil graph on paper, recording the engine's operation. Engineers could adjust valves and steam pressure accordingly to make the engine more efficient. Watt also found a way to regulate the speed of an engine automatically, instead of depending on human hands to open and close pressure valves. His regulator, called a governor, was the first to be widely used, and it would pave the way for future innovations in automated machines.

Between 1790 and 1800, more steams engines were produced than in the entire century before. In 1800, James Watt retired from Boulton & Watt, and his patent expired. His engine was now fair game for other inventors and manufacturers to improve upon and reproduce. Watt had moved steam technology so far ahead that in the following century, it would transform not only manufacturing, but also land and sea travel, commerce, communication, and agriculture. The Industrial Revolution, powered by steam, would move people into a faster, busier, and more city-centered life than ever before.

Early steam engines could be dangerous. Undetected corrosion, bad repairs, or failure to keep water to the required level could cause overheating and boiler explosions. A safety device for steam engines was introduced in 1803, but few manufacturers included it on their engines due to extra cost and the general lack of responsibility for employees that was prevalent in the early days of industry. It wasn't until 1882 that the British government introduced safety regulations. By then, hundreds of workers had perished in boiler accidents.

4 STEAM LOCOMOTION

From 1800 on, steam engines played a central part in the production of goods, both in Great Britain and elsewhere. More people migrated to the cities, looking for work and finding it in noisy, dangerous, steam-driven factories, full of belts and gears that connected engines to machines. While steam was powering more and more mill and shop work, a new generation of inventors was hatching schemes to put steam engines to work elsewhere.

As early as the 1760s, one enterprising Frenchman named Nicolas-Joseph Cugnot built what many consider the world's first automobile. Cugnot had already experimented with turning reciprocating piston action into rotary motion. In 1765, Cugnot put his experiment into action in the form of a heavy, steam-powered vehicle designed to haul cannons.

In 1769, Cugnot produced an improved version of his "steam wagon" that could pull 4 tons (3.6 metric tons) at a speed of about 2.5 miles (4 kilometers) per hour. Cugnot used two wheels in the back of the wagon and one in the front that supported the steam boiler. He steered the vehicle with a tiller,

▼ *This 1770 etching of a steam engine, designed by Nicolas-Joseph Cugnot, illustrates the crash that occurred when he demonstrated his "steam wagon."*

or lever, rather than a wheel. Unfortunately, this first automobile got into the first automobile accident when it crashed into a brick wall.

Catch Me Who Can

People continued to explore ideas for vehicles that could "go without horses." It was not until 1801 that someone actually produced a functioning road **locomotive** (train) powered by steam. On Christmas Eve of that year, Richard Trevithick took seven friends for a ride in his steam locomotive, the Puffing Devil. Trevithick had been experimenting with models of steam locomotives for some time. His locomotive, however, could travel only short distances (less than a mile) before it ran out of steam, which made it impractical for commercial use.

It took another three years for Trevithick to produce the world's first steam locomotive that ran on rails. On this machine, he vented the steam from the engine up the boiler's chimney. This produced a draft that kept the fire burning hot enough around the boiler so that steam pressure would remain high. This locomotive used a single, vertical cylinder, a **flywheel** (a mechanism that kept the piston's action even), and a long **piston rod**. Reaching speeds of nearly 5 miles (8 km) an hour, Trevithick carried 10 tons (9 metric tons) of iron, seventy passengers, and five wagons on a 9-mile (14.5 km) journey. Once again, the locomotive turned out to be impractical, this time because its weight kept breaking the cast-iron rails.

Trevithick's last experiment in locomotion produced a locomotive he named *Catch Me Who Can*. In 1808, he ran the machine on a circular rail he had built for the purpose. The locomotive reached the amazing speed, for the time, of 12 miles (19 km) per hour. It, too, broke the rails, and Trevithick's adventure in

Fast Fact

When Richard Trevithick wanted to show his locomotive to the citizens of London, he charged people five shillings to watch his invention go around a circular track housed inside an enclosure. Although this was about half an average workingman's weekly salary, hundreds of people paid to view this exciting invention.

steam locomotion came to an end. At the same time, however, ads appeared in London papers describing another steam engine that would "run against any mare, horse or gelding that may be produced." Clearly, locomotion was on its way.

The Father of Locomotion

Trevithick's experiments, although unsuccessful, provided a first step for inventors and engineers who had a vision for steam-powered locomotion. Although steam automobiles were a curiosity, they did not capture enough interest to become an industry. As with stationary steam engines, interest in developing steam locomotives was strongest in the mining regions of Great Britain. Not only did the miners need to drain the mines of groundwater and raise the ores and coal they mined to the surface, they also needed to transport the material to its buyers. There was great demand for coal, especially. Coal was used to heat people's homes and, with the development of new technology, for industrial fuel. It powered glass-making factories, metal forges, and the many textile mills being built around the country. The coal mining businesses, or **collieries**, wanted cheaper, faster ways of delivering their product.

Collieries loaded their coal into open carts that were pulled by horses along wooden or cast-iron tracks, called tramways. By 1812, an English inventor named John Blenkinsop had developed a two-cylinder steam locomotive that could run on the tracks. Four Blenkinsop locomotives were soon doing the work formerly done by fifty strong horses.

▼ *George Stephenson improved upon the locomotive design and in 1829, introduced* The Rocket, *pictured below. The* Rocket *was the first steam locomotive to sucessfully pull passenger and freight cars at a reasonable speed.*

The Steam Engine

George Stephenson probably did more than anyone else, however, to push steam locomotion toward the railroad system we know today. In 1814, Stephenson ran his first steam locomotive with **flanged wheels** on cast-iron tracks. The flanges were rims added to the outside edges of the wheels. They made the wheels stronger and kept them on the tracks of the tramway.

In 1825, the Stockton and Darlington Railroad, with Stephenson as its chief engineer, opened as the first public railroad to use locomotives. Unlike earlier railroads, this one used wrought-iron rails that would hold up better than the earlier cast-iron rails, which were weak and brittle. Stephenson built the first locomotive (called the Locomotion) to run on the Stockton and Darlington Railroad.

A Web of Iron

Over the next twelve years, Great Britain laid 500 miles (808 km) of railroad track. By 1852, there were more than 7,500 miles (12,000 km) of track across the small country. Locomotive building, meanwhile, had blossomed into an industry. Railroad engineers and laborers from Britain built railroads all around the world, in Asia, Africa, Europe, and the United States.

Building a web of iron presented many challenges. Railroad workers needed to build sturdy rail beds that would hold up under the weight and friction of the heavy locomotives. They had to dig tunnels through mountains, design trains that could climb steep hills, and construct strong railroad bridges to send the locomotives steaming across rivers and chasms.

The United States faced its own unique challenges. The territory over which American tracks were laid called for some sharp curves that British locomotives

George Stephenson (1781–1848)

George Stephenson was born in England in 1781. At fourteen, he went to work for a coal-mining business. By the age of nineteen, he had advanced to the job of engineman, which meant he took care of the mine's steam engines. Stephenson's experiments and innovations over the years allowed him to build successful steam engines and produce the first railroad to operate completely without animal power. He eventually became chief engineer of six railroad lines, all the while continuing his improvements to steam locomotives. George Stephenson died in 1848 at the age of sixty-seven.

The *Tom Thumb*, produced by Peter Cooper, a New York merchant with an interest and investment in steam power, was the most famous steam locomotive of the new American railroad iindustry. Cooper unveiled his little locomotive in 1830 in order to convince investors that steam power would continue to be important in the future. The train's initial trip was 13 miles (21 km) and took one and one-quarter hours. It was seen as a huge success.

PETER COOPER'S "TOM THUMB" 1829-30 BALTIMORE & OHIO R. R.

▲ *On its first success-ful trial run, Peter Cooper's* Tom Thumb *ran between Baltimore and Ellicott's Mills, Maryland, in August 1830. The steam engine pictured here was attached to an open-air passenger car.*

could not easily handle. So American engineers designed and built their own locomotives. Because they wanted more speed and power, they increased the size of the boilers and the cylinders and raised the steam pressure. They added slanted frames called cowcatchers to the front of locomotives to move objects off the tracks in front of the train (sometimes actual cows or buffalo). To prevent fires, they redesigned smokestacks with a curve at the top to catch sparks from the engines' boilers.

In 1869, a rail line built by the Union Pacific Railroad Company from California met the Central Pacific Railroad Company line built from the East, creating the country's first transcontinental railroad. Such long-distance railroads would create cities, such as Chicago, where only prairies, mountains, and deserts had been. Telegraph lines were strung all along the railroad lines, making almost instant communication possible across the country. Trains routinely added mail cars as well, so letters and messages that might have taken months could travel in just days. By 1900, more than one million Americans worked for the railroads, tending 1.4 million freight cars and thirty-five thousand passenger cars. By 1920, one-third of the world's railroad tracks crisscrossed the United States.

The Price of Steam Rail Travel

As wonderful as they were, however, the railroads also presented some terrible dangers. High-pressure boilers could explode, causing injury and disastrous loss of life. When rails broke, trains could derail with similar results. Because trains traveled fast and far, collisions between trains or with other objects (or people) on the tracks were always a hazard. Just bringing the enormous iron machine to a stop could pose a challenge to the brakemen responsible for this task. Brakemen also had the risky job of coupling (joining) and uncoupling train cars as they moved. An estimated sixty-five thousand American brakemen died on the job between 1870 and 1900. American inventors, like those across the sea, saw these problems as opportunities to create solutions. They replaced the breakable iron tracks with harder rails made of steel. George Westinghouse invented a system of air brakes that would stop all the cars of a train at once without danger to crew or passengers. Eli Janney invented an automatic coupling device.

Steam locomotives continued to run the railroads of the world until the arrival of locomotives that ran on diesel fuel (a fuel refined from petroleum but heavier than gasoline) and, later, electricity. Where diesel was hard to come by, and electricity impractical, steam locomotion continued to be used. There are remote places in the world even today where steam continues to fuel the railroad.

Bells and Whistles

Before radios, the people who ran steam locomotives needed to find ways to communicate so they could avoid collisions and other dangers. Steam itself provided one solution in the form of whistles. Using a code of long and short toots on the steam whistle, engineers could communicate from one train to another. They could also make contact with train workers in other parts of a long train, announcing "The train is stopped," "The train is about to move," or "The train came apart!" Even animals and people on the ground might get a message with one long, loud blast that meant "Get off the tracks!" In today's busy, congested communities, train whistles still continue to alert people that a train is coming. Electric whistles remind people on the train platform to stand back away from the tracks, and they warn drivers to keep their cars safely behind safety barriers at railroad crossings. Some neighborhoods have protested train whistles as a noise nuisance, but most people believe that safety features far outweigh any inconvenience.

5 STEAM NAVIGATION

As time passed, steam inventions continued to develop as solutions to practical problems that no one had been able to solve before. People in the United States found steam engines just as exciting and useful as the British did. They imported British engines for their growing textile industries, and they quickly designed their own versions of the steam locomotive to push back the American frontier. Americans' earliest ideas about steam power, however, focused on moving boats.

When Europeans arrived in America as colonists in the early 1600s, they faced a sparsely populated, wild environment. Two oceans separated them from their homelands. Vast woodlands, thick undergrowth, and mountainous terrain made settlement and travel a

▼ *John Fitch (1743–1798) completed the first successful trial of a steamboat on August 22, 1787, years before Robert Fulton. His 45-foot (14-m) boat traveled along the Delaware River as members of the Constitutional Convention stood on the riverbank watching it go by.*

challenge. Without the help of established cities or well-used roads, the colonists turned to the continent's many great rivers and its lengthy seacoasts to travel and to ship and receive goods. It is not surprising that they imagined steam could be used to improve their ability to travel by water.

First Attempts

The Americans were not the first people to experiment with steam **navigation**. Early records show that a Spanish inventor named Blasco de Garay claimed to use steam to move a vessel in 1543, and Denis Papin proposed that his piston engine might turn paddle wheels to propel a boat. At least two English inventors in the early 1700s obtained patents for boats that would employ a Newcomen engine. One envisioned the engine jetting water out the back of the boat (hydraulic propulsion) to propel it forward. The other devised a plan involving a paddle wheel connected by belts to the engine.

In 1753, the French Academy, an organization devoted to the advancement of science in France, offered a prize for the best plan to move a boat without wind. The winner proposed a propeller-driven boat, but he expected animal power to turn the propeller, not an engine. In 1783, another French inventor, Claude Jouffroy d'Abbans, built a small steamboat that actually worked.

American efforts at steam navigation began in 1760 with a trip by William Henry to England, where he saw steam engines in operation. Three years later, back home in Pennsylvania, Henry built a steam engine, which he installed in a boat equipped with paddle wheels. Although his design failed, it showed others what might be possible.

John Fitch of Connecticut obtained patents in several states for a steam-powered boat with paddle wheels and by 1787 had succeeded in building one that worked. At about the same time, James Rumsey used steam-powered hydraulic propulsion to move a boat up the Potomac River in Maryland. Rumsey's boat achieved a speed of 4 miles (6.4 km) an hour.

Oliver Evans (1755–1819)

Oliver Evans was born in Delaware in 1755, the same year that America's first steam engine was fired up. Working as a millwright, planning and building mills and their machinery, he designed the first fully automated mill for grinding flour. In 1786 he sought a patent for a steam-powered wagon. He did not obtain the patent, but he built a steam engine anyway, designing one that could fit into a vehicle. His high-pressure Columbian engine would power most of America's steamboats and propel the country into power-driven industry. Evans published a book on milling and, in 1805, one on steam engines. He died a wealthy man in 1819 at the age of sixty-four.

John Fitch (1743-1798) grew up in the British colony of Connecticut. While exploring the Ohio River Valley as an adult, he was captured by Native Americans. For years after his release, Fitch had nightmares of Indians chasing him down the river. Inspired by his dreams, Fitch's first steamboat design featured a moving rack of paddles like those on an Indian canoe, rather than the typical paddle wheel seen on later models.

The race to invent a practical steamboat, although a slow one by today's standards, was on.

In 1804, Oliver Evans patented his Columbian steam engine. This engine was smaller than its British counterparts. It was also cheaper to build, easier to run, and simpler to take care of. Its higher steam pressure made it more dangerous, because it was more subject to explosions, but this also suited it to use in land vehicles and boats.

In 1805, Evans attached his steam engine to a boat and mounted the whole thing on wheels. Propelling the vehicle with the steam engine, he drove it through the streets of Philadelphia, Pennsylvania, and finally to the Schuylkill River, showing that steam power would work on the road and the water. Even today, some people consider it the first steam-powered amphibious vehicle in America. Evans proceeded to establish a business he called Mars Works to build his steam engines. Evans's Columbian engine would soon become the favored engine for steam-powered boats used on America's rivers.

Highways of Water

As Americans migrated into the heartland of the continent, rivers provided their best avenue for travel and commerce. The Mississippi River, especially, was a vital trade route. The river's current ran north to south, which meant that products such as iron ore, lumber, salt pork, and whiskey could be floated downstream on barges with the current to propel them. The route north, however, was much more difficult and expensive, since it depended upon packhorses and small riverboats. A boat that could be successfully powered upstream against the river's current was desperately needed.

Robert Fulton rose up to meet this challenge. By far the most successful of America's steamboat inventors, Fulton tested his first steamboat on the Hudson River in 1807. The *Clermont* made the trip from New York to Albany and back in an astonishing thirty-two hours, traveling against the current at 5 miles (8 km) per hour. One witness described the boat as "a monster moving on the waters, defying wind and tide, and breathing flames and smoke." Fulton used a Watt double-action engine in which he burned pinewood rather than coal. The engine turned a crank on a paddle-wheel shaft, and the paddle wheel propelled the boat.

Fulton continued to design and build steamboats for use on rivers. In partnership with Robert Livingston, he obtained exclusive rights to navigate the rivers of New York and the lower Mississippi River. Fulton's large steamboat, the *New Orleans*, ran into trouble navigating the Ohio River because of shallows and river debris. It eventually completed its trip south, but when it turned to steam back upriver, it could not fight the current. The large, inland rivers had strong currents and were typically dotted with sandbars, tree trunks, and debris that smaller boats could easily bypass. It was clear that the future of steam boating itself had hit a snag.

Once again, the inventive imagination and spirit came to the rescue, this time in the person of Henry Miller Shreve. After watching one of Fulton's steamboats run into the shallows of the Mississippi River, Shreve launched a career of designing better steamboats for river use. Eventually, he designed a "snag boat." This steamboat was equipped with a special front end fitted to pull up tree trunks and other "snags" as it went. Shreve's snag boats were

Robert Fulton (1765–1815)

Robert Fulton was born in Pennsylvania in 1765. At seventeen, he left home to study painting and book publishing. In 1786, he traveled to London, where he pursued a growing interest in engineering. He studied how to design and build canals, which were a major part of commercial transportation. His designs for improving canals and bridges played an important role in the construction of the Erie Canal. In 1801, Fulton successfully developed a diving boat, an early version of a submarine. By 1807, he had launched his first successful riverboat driven by steam. He established a regular steamboat and freight service along the Mississippi River by 1814, the same year he presented his design for the first steam-propelled warship. Fulton died of pneumonia at the age of fifty.

able to clear miles and miles of inland rivers, greatly improving their use for navigation. Maintaining rivers became an important business as commercial ports sprang up all along the great rivers of the nation. Snag boats are still in use today to clear environmental debris and pollution deposited along continuously changing riverbeds.

Ships at Sea

The steamboat's ability to travel regardless of wind and weather made this type of vessel attractive to seagoers as well as riverboaters. A sailing ship could easily become becalmed for lack of wind or sent hopelessly off-course by a storm. A steamboat, on the other hand, would stay its course. In 1809, Colonel John Stevens put the idea of steam-powered sea travel to the test. He took his steamboat *Phoenix* on a 13-mile (21-km) sea voyage from Hoboken, New Jersey,

▼ *This sketch of an early boiler engine built by John Stevens, a rival of Robert Fulton, shows the twin screws used on a steamboat engine. Stevens's machine, rebuilt in 1805 with some improvements, is still in existence today.*

The Steam Engine

to Philadelphia, Pennsylvania, catching the attention of steamboat enthusiasts on both sides of the Atlantic Ocean.

After ten years of voyages that hugged the coast, in 1819, Americans made the world's first transatlantic steam voyage in the *Savannah*. They ran out of coal by the time they reached Ireland and had to return under sail, but in 1838, the British *Sirius* completed a round-trip, transatlantic voyage entirely by steam. By 1850, the typical thirty-five-day transatlantic trip of a sailing vessel took just over eighteen days by steam. In Europe, steamers used for coastal and ferry purposes were transporting tens of thousands of passengers a year.

The *Sirius* was the first steamship to have a surface condenser. This invention allowed a steamship to use the same supply of freshwater over and over again in the steam engine cycle, rather than having to take on seawater that might damage the boiler. More innovations followed. Iron replaced wood on many steamships' hulls. A **screw propeller**, a device that looks like an electric fan, began to take the place of the wooden paddle wheels, which were easily damaged. At the same time, engineers developed steam engines that weighed less and had greater numbers of smaller cylinders with faster piston action.

Steam-powered sea vessels seemed to put the whole world on the move. New companies opened up steamship lines to cover oceanic routes around the globe, and people migrated across the seas in huge numbers. As the world steamed toward the twentieth century, anything connected to steam power seemed possible. Inventive minds never stopped dreaming. Technology, steam and otherwise, was about to take a giant leap forward.

Fast Fact

The *Sirius* was actually racing with another steamship in her first nonstop voyage across the Atlantic. The *Sirius* left Ireland on April 3, 1838, and arrived in New York eighteen days later. The next day, a ship called *Great Western*, which had left Ireland four days after the *Sirius*, also arrived in New York, breaking the Sirius' shortly held crossing record by three days.

6 MAKING THE STEAM ENGINE BETTER

▼ *The March 1862 battle between the Confederate* Merrimack *(pictured below) and the Union army's* Monitor *transformed naval warfare. This first battle between ironclad steamships signaled the end of the wooden ship in combat.*

In Great Britain, the mills, factories, railways, and shipping lines continued their successful conversion to steam power.

In the United States, it was war that made steam a part of everyday life. The United States depended heavily on manufactured goods from Britain. The War of 1812 between Britain and the United States cut off the flow of imports from British manufacturers, causing a shortage of all sorts of goods. The need for these products pushed U.S. manufacturers firmly into the steam age. Cotton, lumber, and flour mills, gunpowder and woolens factories, paint and barrel manufacturers, glassworks, and other businesses all converted to steam power.

From the mid-1800s through the turn of the century, steam remained the industrial world's chief source of power. By 1838, the United States had 250 companies devoted to building steam engines. American producers concentrated on developing engines that ran on high pressure and eliminated condensers. Soon, they were exporting U.S. steam engines to Cuba and South America. U.S. manufacturers further improved the steam engine

business by creating standards that all steam engine builders would use. This meant that parts could be interchanged from one company's engine to another. It also meant that some businesses could simply make steam engine parts instead of whole engines.

Steam Engines on Parade

In 1876, the city of Philadelphia hosted a centennial exhibition featuring steam technology. The exhibition hall itself, called Machinery Hall, extended over 13 acres (5 hectares) and included dozens of engine-run machines. The star of the show, however, was the Corliss Centennial Engine.

At the time of the exhibition, the Corliss Centennial Engine was the largest steam engine in the world. George H. Corliss had designed the engine to have the power and efficiency to run all the machinery in the exhibition hall simultaneously. The Corliss engine stood 45 feet (13.7 m) tall with a flywheel that weighed 56 tons (51 metric tons) and was 30 feet (9 m) in diameter. For the opening ceremony, U.S. president Ulysses Grant and Brazilian emperor Dom Pedro each pulled a lever, which started the huge steam engine's action. Immediately, 13 acres of machines started up, combing wool, tearing hemp, sewing cloth, spinning cotton, printing newspapers, sawing logs, making shoes, lithographing wallpaper, manufacturing envelopes, and pumping water.

The Traction Engine

Inventors and business innovators like Corliss saw steam power as a way to turn the wheels of what was later called the Industrial Revolution. At the same time, ordinary people with everyday jobs,

George H. Corliss 1817–1888

George H. Corliss was born in New York in 1817. By 1846, he was a partner in an engine-building company called Fairbanks, Bancroft & Company. There he invented a steam engine regulated by a special, improved valve gear. In 1856, Corliss founded what would become the world's largest producer of steam engines, the Corliss Steam Engine Company of Providence, Rhode Island. During the Civil War, the Corliss Company provided some of the steam engine parts needed by the ironclad battleship *Monitor* of the Union army. By the time Corliss died in 1888, he had obtained sixty-eight patents and made huge contributions to the practices of **mass production** and **standardization**.

▲ *At Philadelphia's centennial exhibition in 1876, the success of the Corliss engine, which symbolized the fighting, inventive spirit of the hundred-year-old nation, filled Americans with great pride. The Corliss engine was in use for the next thirty years.*

especially farmers, began to appreciate what steam could do for them. The earliest farm to use steam power (in 1798) was English. The farmer was also an engineer and ironmaster, and he ran a threshing machine using an engine similar to the ones Richard Trevithick had built.

By the mid-1800s, inventors and engineers had figured out how to make portable engines that were light enough to be hauled by horses over farm fields without bogging down. Such engines powered threshing machines, helped to clear fields, and pulled plows and cultivators. Farmers in Britain and the United States continued to use these engines to steam-power all kinds of farm work as late as the 1950s.

Traction engines were also designed for hauling heavy equipment that weighed up to 120 tons (109 metric tons). Engineers fitted them with three-speed gears for running on paved roads. Extra water tanks allowed the engines to travel farther before the boiler would need a water stop. Showmen who ran traveling fairs used such engines, dressing them up with brass fittings and shiny paint. These road locomotives would haul the fair rides from place to place, then power the rides and provide lights. Steam tractors, which weighed less than 5 tons (4.5 metric tons) and burned less fuel, were used for hauling lighter loads.

Steamrollers, designed specifically to roll out new roadways, started out as very heavy steam traction engines weighing as much as 30 tons (27 metric tons). All that weight, however, did not make the

The Steam Engine

rollers work efficiently, so engineers tried new, lighter, and smaller designs. Modernized steamrollers were still in use as late as the 1960s.

The Steam Turbine

Surprisingly, even though steam was vital to progress in industry, agriculture, communication, and travel, it had a relatively short life as the primary source of engine power. By the end of the 1800s, even the vastly improved traditional steam engines of the Industrial Revolution began to decrease in their importance to countries in Europe and North America.

Improved technology and understanding were changing the way people could generate power of all sorts. Better, more accurate tools led to new ideas and new inventions. Inventors developed an internal combustion engine that used gas or oil fuel directly. They also learned how to use water directly for hydraulic power instead of having to heat it up first to make steam. These power sources were less dangerous and much more efficient than the steam engine.

The single greatest change in technology was the development of electricity in the late 1800s. When

Steam for Fun

Steam power was obviously serious business. That did not stop people, though, from putting it to use for fun as well. By the 1870s, fairgrounds featured steam-powered merry-go-rounds, small-scale trains for "scenic rides," and a variety of other engine-driven rides for the pleasure of the fairgoers. Music sounded throughout the fairgrounds, whistling out of the pipes of a calliope (pronounced kah-**lie**-uh-pee). A calliope is a keyboard instrument similar to an organ. Its music, however, is created by steam that is piped through the instrument's whistles. Such steam-powered entertainments continued to attract crowds until after World War I (1914–1918) and are still used in some circus parades today.

The first calliope was invented by Joseph Stoddard of Worcester, Massachusetts, in 1815. It consisted of fifteen different-sized whistles attached to the top of a steam boiler. The whistles were hit by a series of pins attached to a revolving cylinder. The cylinder was later replaced with a keyboard that had wires attached to the valves on the boiler, enabling the player to operate the instrument like a piano.

Thomas Edison patented his incandescent light bulb, he created an efficient, versatile form of power that had endless applications. Much of the industrial work done by steam engines would soon be electrified. First, though, electricity would have to be delivered to every city, town, home, and business. To do that required the generation of electricity on a grand scale.

The need for electrical generation plants did more than anything else to move steam as a power source into the twentieth century. Electrical generation plants used a power source to create electrical current that could be delivered to customers. Some plants used waterpower, but that depended on a constant, plentiful source of water, such as a strong river nearby. Early on, some generation plants employed steam **reciprocating engines**. However, the steam engines could not be made to run fast enough to be effective and efficient. Large steam engines developed serious problems of vibration. The larger the steam engine, the greater the vibration.

Inventors had experimented for a long time with a **steam turbine** in order to find more efficiency in the expanding properties of steam. The steam turbine used steam for power differently than the engine did. Steam turbines were more efficient because they were able to capture the power of steam through every phase of its expansion. A steam engine had to wait for the steam to build up a great amount of pressure and then utilize it. In a steam turbine, steam is pro-pelled directly onto blades, or vanes, of a revolving wheel. The force of the steam hits the blades and impels the wheel to turn, which in turn creates power. The steam turbine has great advantages over the reciprocating engine. A smaller unit can deliver more power with less vibration, it has much greater fuel efficiency because it operates in a more direct way, and it can run at superhigh speed.

It was not until 1884 that British inventor Charles Algernon Parsons (1854–1931) built the first successful steam turbine. Although many had tried before him, the turbine required technological advances that simply had not existed earlier. In fact, many people did not take Parsons's turbine seriously until he demonstrated a 100-foot (30.5 m) turbine-propelled boat in 1897. The *Turbinia* flew across the water at 35 nautical miles (about 40 miles) an hour, much faster than the fastest ships in the British navy fleet.

Like so many inventions before it, the steam turbine, once successfully demonstrated, caught the interest of many inventors, engineers, and investors. In 1895, an American named Charles Gordon Curtis (1860–1936) patented the Curtis multiple-stage steam turbine. Curtis's turbine was designed in such a way that it could use the expansion of steam at its high-pressure phase, its moderate-pressure phase, and its low-pressure phase by linking several turbines together. The Curtis multistage steam turbine was bought by General Electric in 1901 and improved over time by a growing army of electrical engineers. It would be used to power not only electric power plants but great seagoing ships as well.

Use of the steam turbine continues in the twenty-first century. It accounts for 75 percent of electrical generation in the United States today, in plants powered by fossil fuel, natural gas, and nuclear energy. While the turbine is not technically a steam engine, it is certainly steam power in its latest, greatest phase.

▼ *This 1894 photograph shows the SS* Turbinia, *designed by Charles Parsons, under way with flags flying. The success of Parsons's ship sparked interest in the use of steam turbines for marine passage.*

7

INTO THE FUTURE

O ne of the most pressing challenges our modern, automated world now faces is the need for power without pollution. Much of the fuel used to power the engines in such everyday necessities as cars, trucks, trains, planes, home heating systems, and, especially, electric power plants comes from nonrenewable sources called **fossil fuels**. Coal, natural gas, oil, and fuels made from oil are natural resources we mine from our planet Earth. World demand, however, is using up the existing supplies of these fuels. They will not last forever.

Our challenge is to burn less fossil fuel so it lasts longer or, ideally, to use other sources of power. This means developing engines that are more efficient or that run well on other sorts of power, such as sun, water, or, more controversially, nuclear reactions.

Another major concern for people today is a clean environment. When fuels such as coal or gasoline are consumed to run engines, the gases left over after burning them for energy are harmful to our environment. If scientists can find a way to use more of

▼ *The burning of fossil fuels releases pollutants into the environment, causing damage to land, air, and seas. This photograph shows the effect of acid rain on trees. Acid rain is precipitation that becomes acidic due to pollutants in the atmosphere.*

the fuel in the burning process, less fuel would be needed, because less would be wasted. In addition, with less of the fuel left unburned, fewer pollutants would be released into the environment. Sun and water energy sources are not polluting, but nuclear energy, while "clean" burning in the short run, leaves nuclear waste that is difficult to dispose of and can be highly toxic to the environment for tens of thousands of years.

Steam Power at Home

One idea that today's inventors and engineers are exploring is the possibility of running homes on their own generators, powered by steam. Skip Goebel, founder of a company called Sensible Steam Consultants, is working on a design for a practical, home-scale steam generator system. His design uses wood to feed the boiler. This steam generator would not burn wood the way it is burned in a fireplace, with an open flame and a lot of smoke going up the chimney. Instead, the system would burn the gas released from wood when it is superheated but not given the oxygen it needs to make an open flame. If Goebel's design can be made into a practical steam generator, people will be able to produce all the electricity they need from home without burning fossil fuel or polluting. It would, however, require wood, which is already being over logged in many parts of the world.

Steam Power on the Roads

Steam power ran the earliest cars and trucks people used for transportation. Gas-burning engines, though, turned out to be cheaper, easier to run, quieter, and

Fast Fact

In 1942, *New Steam Age: The Magazine of Modern Steam Power* debuted. One of its lead articles discussed the ongoing quest to develop an efficient steam-powered automobile and featured preliminary design plans for such a car. More than fifty years later, that quest continues.

more powerful. People traded in the steam vehicles, with their awkward boilers and belching smokestacks, for the sleeker, gas-burning models.

Today, inventors are rethinking that choice. The cost of gas and oil has risen dramatically. Our fuel supply depends not only on how much fossil fuel is left in the ground, but also on whether the countries with large fuel supplies are friendly to the countries that need the fuel.

Engineers from one company in Germany are presently testing a new steam engine that may bring steam vehicles back to the roads. The steam engine uses a "porous burner." The porous burner is a block with small holes. Like Goebel's home generator, it has the ability to burn fuel without an open flame. It can also burn a variety of different fuels, including natural gas and gasoline. While these are nonrenewable fuels that tend to pollute, this engine produces much less pollution because it consumes most of the fuel.

The German engineers working on this car claim that it is a powerful vehicle able to travel 40 miles (64 km) on a gallon of fuel, as opposed to some cars today that get less than 20 miles (32 km). The engineers still need to experiment. They don't know yet how to keep the steam engine's water from freezing in winter. They also want to find a way to make the engine start as quickly as a conventional engine.

Steam on the Rails

As with cars, railroad companies replaced their steam locomotives when diesel-fueled trains were invented. In the 1980s, oil fuel prices rose steadily, costing big burners of diesel fuel, such as the railroad companies, a lot of money. In the interest of saving

The Steam Engine

money, they began to rethink the old steam locomotives of a hundred years earlier. A number of companies in the United States, England, Germany, South Africa, Zimbabwe, and Switzerland began experimenting with new ways to make steam locomotives that would eliminate the high prices of diesel fuel by burning coal or other fuels.

The new steam locomotives that engineers began designing would make huge improvements on the old designs. Among other changes, they would concentrate on replacing the old steam reciprocating engines with steam turbines. They would also use computer technology to make the turbine run at the highest and safest efficiency possible. Before these companies could put their new ideas into action, however, fuel prices fell. Once again, it was easier and cheaper for the railroads to keep the old diesel-powered locomotives running rather than investing in brand-new locomotives.

Today, people are once again considering updated steam-driven locomotives. Like many early steam inventions, the ideas have not developed quickly. One company in Japan, called Mitsui, already has all

▲ *This photograph shows a section of the engine of the Union Pacific's* Challenger No. 3985, *built in 1943. It is the largest and most powerful steam locomotive in the world today.* Challenger No. 3985 *was retired in 1962 and restored in 1981. It is currently used for exhibition purposes around the nation. Its permanent home is in Cheyenne, Wyoming.*

the parts available to manufacture a steam turbine locomotive. What the company lacks is a customer to buy the product. When people feel a strong enough need to replace the traditional diesel-electric trains, the steam turbine trains are very likely to become reality.

Steam Power from Planet Earth

The problem of how to burn less fuel still remains. In the United States, electric power plants burn an enormous amount of fuel to provide enough power for the entire huge and fully automated country. Scientists feel certain that the demands for electricity will only increase.

Inventors and engineers have offered one solution that makes use of **geothermal energy**. Geothermal energy uses the heat beneath the cool surface of the earth. The earth's inner core measures up to 7,600° Fahrenheit (4,200° Celsius). Some power plants in California and Hawaii even now are designed to turn that heat into electric power.

Water can be found deep inside the earth, where the extreme heat of the earth's core heats it up. As the water heats, it circulates back toward the earth's

▼ The Blue Lagoon on the Reykjanes Peninsula in Iceland is a geothermal region where hot water deep inside the earth is circulated back up to the surface. The reservoir is the site of a spa where people bathe in the warm, steamy water.

The Steam Engine

surface, where it forms underground geothermal reservoirs, or lakes. Geothermal power plants use wells to draw the hot water and steam in the reservoirs to the surface and pipe them to a steam turbine generator. Once the energy available in the water and steam has been used, they are cooled and sent back into the earth. There they will heat up again and refill the geothermal reservoirs.

The more scientists learn and the more advanced technology becomes, the better able they'll be to take advantage of geothermal energy. As far as anyone knows, this is an energy source that will never be used up or create environmental damage. What makes it work is the power of steam.

Earth and Beyond

Great ideas for using steam power do not stop on Earth's surface. In 2003, a company called Surrey Satellite Technology Limited launched into outer space a satellite that used a steam propulsion system.

The scientists at the satellite company considered this a successful experiment. They demonstrated that water (and steam) can be used as a safe, inexpensive, effective spacecraft propellant, rather than the more expensive and dangerous chemicals they had relied on in the past. In the process, they joined a long line of people who think steam is one of the good answers to the challenges that people face, both today and into the future.

Steam power seems here to stay. Human beings are endlessly curious about how things work, and they show again and again that they can invent new ways of solving problems and meeting life's challenges. It looks as though steam power will continue to be a part of the solutions they come up with.

The geothermal power plant located at The Geysers, 90 miles (145 km) north of San Francisco, California, is the most successful alternative energy project in history. The power plant built at The Geysers uses a "dry" reservoir, which produces steam but only a small amount of water. Steam is piped directly into the plant to provide power to spin a turbine generator. The Geysers first started producing electricity in 1960.

TIMELINE

1st century A.D.	Hero of Alexandria creates a steam-driven toy.
1602	Giovanni Battista della Porta recognizes that cooling steam creates a vacuum.
1690	Denis Papin's experiments using a piston and cylinder demonstrate the power of steam.
1698	Thomas Savery obtains a patent for the first steam pump.
1712	Thomas Newcomen manufactures his first full-scale steam engine.
1769	Nicholas-Joseph Cugnot builds the world's first steam-powered automobile. James Watt obtains a patent for an improved atmospheric steam engine.
1787	John Fitch completes a successful trial of a steamboat on the Delaware River.
1801	Richard Trevithick takes friends for a ride in his locomotive *Puffing Devil*.
1805	Oliver Evans attaches his Columbian steam engine to a boat.
1807	Robert Fulton tests his first steamboat, the *Clermont*, on the Hudson River.
1814	George Stephenson runs the first steam locomotive with flanged wheels on railroad tracks.
1825	The Stockton and Darlington Railroad, the first public railroad to use locomotives, begins operation.
1830	Peter Cooper's *Tom Thumb* locomotive convinces investors that steam power is the way of the future.
1838	The British steamship *Sirius* completes the first round-trip, transatlantic, steam-powered voyage.
1869	The Union Pacific Railroad meets the Central Pacific Railroad creating America's first transcontinental railroad.
1876	Philadelphia hosts a centennial exhibition featuring the Corliss engine.
1884	Charles Algernon Parsons builds the first successful steam turbine.
1895	Charles Gordon Curtis patents the multistage steam turbine.
1900	1.4 million freight cars and 35,000 passenger cars transport people and goods across the United States annually.
1920	One-third of the world's railroad tracks are laid in America.
1943	Union Pacific builds the *Challenger No. 3985*, the most powerful steam locomotive in the world.
1980's	Oil prices in the United States soar as supply dries up, renewing interest in steam-powered energy generation.
Today	Steam turbines account for 75 percent of electrical generation in the U.S.

GLOSSARY

colliery: a coal mine and the buildings around it

cylinder: the stationary engine chamber that surrounds the movable piston

energy: the ability to do work (found in chemical, electrical, heat, light, mechanical, and nuclear forms)

engine: a machine for converting energy into mechanical force and motion

flanged wheels: wheels with rims that attach them to rails

flywheel: a heavy wheel used with a reciprocating engine to make the motion of the piston steady and regular

fossil fuel: any fuel that is formed underground from the remains of animals and plants, such as coal, natural gas, or oil

geothermal energy: energy created by using the heat of the earth's interior

locomotive: a self-propelled vehicle, such as one that runs on rails

machine: an instrument designed to transfer power or forceto do specific work

mass production: production of goods in great quantity instead of one at a time

mechanical work: the energy transferred in applying force over a distance

navigation: the work of getting ships from place to place

patent: a legal document that prevents people from stealing or making money from another persons idea or inventions

piston: a short cylinder that moves within a cylindrical chamber

piston rod: a rod that connects the motion of the piston to the rest of the engine

pressure: the application of force to something

reciprocating engine: engines that are run by action of pistons

screw propeller: a fan-like device that is used to make a boat or airplane move ahead

standardization: a system that sets the measurements for all parts that perform the same function

steam turbine: an engine that is run by steam jets against blades on a rotating spindle

FOR MORE INFORMATION

Books

Brain, Marshall. *How Stuff Works.* Hoboken, NJ: John Wiley, 2001.

Macaulay, David. *The New Way Things Work.* Boston: Houghton Mifflin, 1998.

Sproule, Anna. *James Watt: Master of the Steam Engine.* Woodbridge, CT: Blackbirch Press 2001.

Tocci, Salvatore. *Experiments with Heat.* New York: Scholastic Library Publishing, 2003.

Videos and DVDs

American Steam. Montreal, Canada: Madacy Entertainment, 2001.

America's Railroads—The Steam Train Legacy. Entertainment Distributing, 2003.

Modern Marvels: Engines. New York: The History Channel, 2003.

Trains Unlimited. Volume 1: Steam Trains/When Giants Roamed. New York: The History Channel, 2003.

Web Sites

en.wikipedia.org/wiki/Steam Encyclopedia description of steam, with Internet links to related subjects.

en.wikipedia.org/wiki/Steam_locomotive Encyclopedia description of steam locomotives, with photographs and Internet links to related subjects.

inventors.about.com/library/inventors/blsteamengine.htm A history of steam engines and their inventors, with Internet links on related subjects.

travel.howstuffworks.com/steam.htm Description and diagrams of how steam engines work.

www.backwoodshome.com/articles/goebel43.html Article by Skip Goebel, founder of a company called Sensible Steam Consultants, on steam power for home use in the future.

www.sapeinsman.com/old_cars/ A history of the first steam automobiles with illustrations.

www.trainweb.org/tusp/21_cent.html Descriptions and diagrams of twenty-first century attempts to use steam for heavy-haul locomotives.

INDEX

Author Biography

Deborah DeFord has written many books about the past and its influence on the way we live today. Her first fictional book for young people, *An Enemy Among Them*, told the story of one colonial family's experiences during the American Revolution. As a writer and editor for the children's magazine, *U*S*Kids*, she authored numerous articles about nature, science, and the way things work. She resides in Connecticut.